Soil of the Soul

Preparing Our Lives
for the Journey Through Lent

by
Rev. Dr. David Mullens
&
C. Curtis Austin

Introduction

The Lenten Season is a 40-day journey of preparation, inner-reflection, and spiritual devotion. Followers of the Christian faith use this time to pray, fast, read, and meditate in an effort to be closer to God. This season allows the seeker of God to walk alongside Jesus, God's Son, as he travels to the Cross, gives himself over to the Grave, and raises victoriously to Life Eternal.

Lent begins with Ash Wednesday and ends on Easter Day. The 40-day count is based on every day except Sundays, which are celebrations of Christ's Resurrection and are not considered days of penitence.

For centuries, the Church has utilized the days leading up to Easter as a time for self-examination and preparation for what many deem as the most Holy Day of the Christian Calendar. We follow this tradition, join with that "great cloud of witnesses" who have gone before, and unite with fellow believers around the world, setting aside this time as an opportunity to reflect, repent and re-order of our souls.

We pray that as you use this daily guide, God will move us in such a way that together, we will embody the life of Christ. This daily devotion is intended to be a gentle reminder of God's love for you; a love that is deeper than any you've ever known. As you read these pages over the season of Lent, may you find yourself closer to the Risen King, reassured in your Faith Journey, and renewed in the Hope and Love of God.

This devotional's overarching theme comes from Matthew 13, when Jesus shares the parable of the soil. Jesus tells of a sower who sows seeds and some of the seeds fell on the path, some fell on rocky soil, some fell on soil where weeds grew up and choked out the life of the plant, but some of the seed fell on good soil where there was a great harvest.

As you journey through Lent, reflect on the soil of your soil. Is your soil conducive to growth? Are there rocks? Weeds?

Use these days of Lent to prepare the soil of your soil.

Suggestions for Using This Devotional

We want to offer a few suggestions which may make the next 40 days more meaningful.

First, find a time that works best for you each day. Some people are early-risers and can focus well before the rest of the world comes alive. Others enjoy a late night after the rest of world has gone to bed. It is important to find a time that suits you and your rhythms. There is no right or wrong, only what will work best for you.

Second, find a place, a location that works for you. You may want to sit at the kitchen table with this guide, your Bible, and a cup of coffee. You may want to land in a comfortable chair where you can put your feet up and relax. Whether you sit in a straight back chair with your feet flat on the floor or find a quiet location in an easy chair, you should be sure to find a comfortable position, but not so comfortable as to induce sleep. You can close your eyes or keep them open depending on which way helps you to quiet yourself.

Third, and perhaps most important, limit distractions. If you live in a busy household, this is a great challenge, indeed. We all live in a world of noise, technology, and distractions: Television, radio, cell phones, to-do lists, and busy schedules call to us non-stop activities. However, these distractions often prevent us from slowing down, unplugging for a short time, and focusing on God's voice. The Creator of the Universe wants to tell us something. We encourage you to stop and hear what that might be!

Finally, be patient. If you've never practiced the discipline of daily devotion, this may be difficult for you at first. Five minutes can seem like an eternity. Give yourself grace.

Think of this daily practice as an exercise for your soul. If you have ever tried to get in better physical shape, you know that those first few days are tough. Even a person who power-walks five miles each day began with a comfortable stroll. The same can be true with devotional living. Start small. Five minutes of devotional focus today may grow to ten minutes next week and a half-hour of deep meditation by the end of the 40-days. The key is to allow yourself time with God. Don't worry about the clock but instead, concentrate on the moment, God's presence, and the voice of God.

Who knows? In the end, you might just find the seed of God's Amazing Grace sprouting in your life!

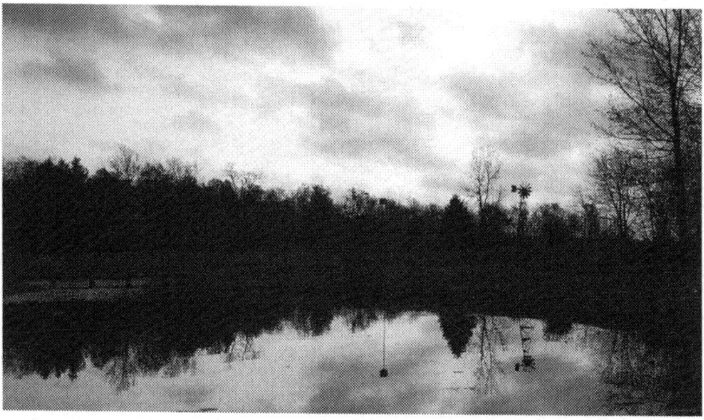

Day 1 – ASH WEDNESDAY
Job 42:1-6

Quiet yourself and your mind. Take three deep breaths. Rest in God's presence. If you need, write down any recurring thoughts on paper and/or a calendar. Remember, this is not just a task to check off your list; you are making time for God to work in your life.

Read today's passage listed above.

Job had a hard life (a major understatement). He lost everything and in the end he became frustrated with God, as most of us would. However, in a moment of understanding and honesty, Job acknowledges his limited ability to understand all of God's ways and commits to trusting God completely. In a covering of dust and ashes, he repents of his pride and turns over control of his life to God.

Historically, the Christian Church begins the Season of Lent with a service of Ash Wednesday. It is not uncommon to see people with the mark of ashes on their forehead later in the day. It is a reminder that, much like Job, we need to enter this season of reflection in humility and repentance.

In light of Job's decision to repent and follow God, think about these two questions:

1. What difficulties am I facing in my life and how have I failed to trust God in the midst of these challenging moments.
2. How can I trust God more?

End your time by praying for the struggles of life and thanking God for his presence in both the good and bad times, even when you don't remember he's there. Feel free to pray, "Father, here I am for you."

Your Reflections

Day 2 – Thursday
Colossians 1:9-10

The Spiritual Life is a gift: God gives. God blesses. We cannot "grow" our spiritual life any more than a farmer can make crops grow. Growth is a gift from a loving God. However, we can create an atmosphere or environment where growth can occur.

Read today's passage listed above. Read it slowly and allow the words to speak to your heart and soul.

Reflect on the verses and think about these questions:
1. How have you grown in the knowledge of God in the past year?
2. How have you come to know God better?
3. What would you need to do in the next year to grow in your faith?

Pray: Almighty God, cause your good gifts to grow in my life, today and every day. AMEN.

Your Reflections

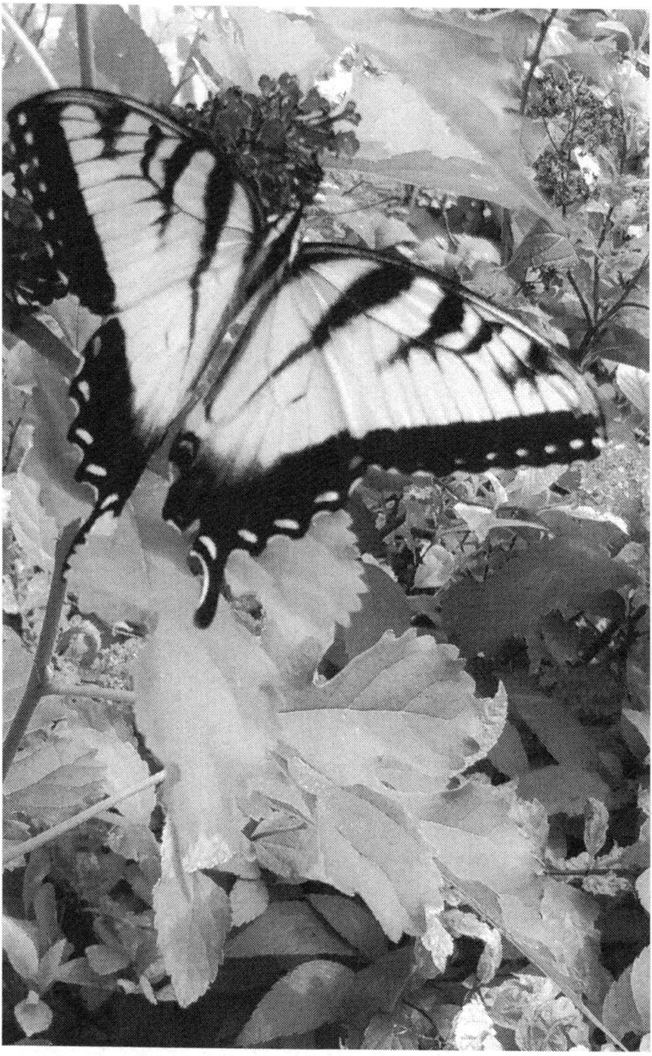

Day 3 – Friday
Psalm 63

Prayer practice: Attention.

You will find "prayer practices" throughout this devotional. Think of a prayer practice as an approach to prayer. Some of these practices might be familiar while others may be new. These prayer practices remind us that there are many ways to pray. We hope you discover practices that resonate with you and become part of your formative journey.

For the first prayer practice you will need a notebook and at least ten minutes. Find a quiet place where you will not be disturbed. Turn off your TV, radio, phone, and anything else that might be distracting.

Take some deep breaths. Breathe in God's Spirit. Exhale your tension and stress.

Spend the next few minutes focusing your attention on God. When a thought comes, don't address it, or think about it, simply "let it be." If you are tempted to give your attention to the thought, simply write it down so you can think about it later. Allow yourself to sit in the presence of God. End this practice by writing a few words describing your experience.

Note: You may find this practice difficult, especially when you first start. Don't give up too quickly. Over time, you may find distractions being minimized and times of silence life-giving.

Your Reflections

Day 4 – Saturday
Galatians 5:22-26

Begin by taking three deep breaths. Close your eyes and envision all that God has done for you. Picture yourself as you think others might see you. Or better, picture yourself as God sees you. Are you kind and loving? Are you forgiving and gracious? Are you generous and giving?

Think about the condition of your spiritual soil? What is the condition of your heart? Has it become hard after years of difficult travel? Is there even a chance that The Great Gardener's seeds can find a hold in your hard heart? What needs to happen in your life over this season of Lent that will allow Love, Grace, Peace, and Forgiveness to take root?

Meditate on these thoughts. Spend time contemplating your life and its direction.

Spend some time praying, asking for God to soften your heart and prepare it for growth and change.

Your Reflections

The 1st Sunday of Lent

Reading: 2 Thessalonians 3:4-5

Hymn: I Am Thine, O Lord
  I am thine, O Lord, I have heard thy voice,
  And it told thy love to me;
  But I long to rise in the arms of faith,
  And be closer drawn to thee.

Reflection: Today is a day to celebrate love and devotion; because it is Sunday! This is the day of the week in which the Church Universal gathers to declare its appreciation for God's amazing gift of life and grace. Jesus gave his life so that you might live. Jesus arose victorious so you might have life everlasting.

Prayer: Take a few minutes to thank God for all the many gifts of your life, especially the Love of God. Allow God to direct your thoughts and be mindful that you remain in a posture of gratitude.

Your Reflections

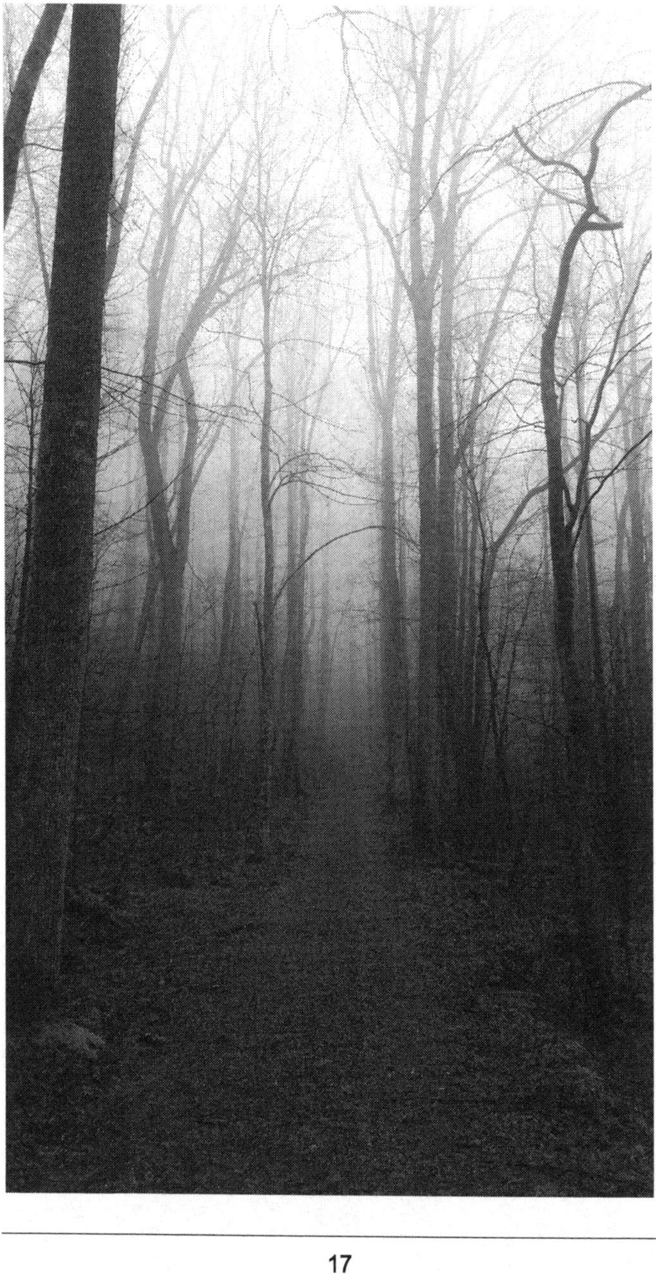

Day 5 – Monday

Reading: Matthew 13:1-9

A few years back I decided to start a garden. I envisioned tomatoes, onions, and peppers growing strong and tall. I dreamed of the wonderful Salsa I would make from the yield of the land.

Since this would be the first garden at our house, I would have to find a good area and prepare the soil. Over the next few days, I used various tools to dig down into the deep rich soil below the hard, grassy surface. Shovel, pick, and hoe were used to break the hard crusty external layer. The work was harder than I anticipated. A few times I wanted to give up, but with thoughts of the produce...and salsa...swirling in my mind, I continued the hard work of preparing the soil.

As I seek to cultivate my life so the seeds of God's grace can grow, I am reminded of my garden. Jesus says that the sower sows, but the seeds don't always produce a harvest. Some fall on the hard path and are whisked away never making an impact. In order for the harvest to come, the seed must be planted in good soil.

Over the years, I've learned that sometimes my soil is hard, sometimes rocky, and sometimes there are weeds everywhere. My task is to cultivate the soil of my soul so God's presence can take shape and form in my life.

Take a few deep breaths and allow any tension and distraction to melt away. You are in God's presence. You always have been in God's presence, but sometimes we forget. Embrace God's presence as you reflect.

How is your soil right now? Hard? Rocky? Weedy? Good? Talk with God.

Your Reflections

Day 6 – Tuesday

Reading: Matthew 13:18-23

Preparing a garden takes work. Tools can help make the work easier, or at least quicker. Since I did not have a rototiller, I had to use hand tools. Some were not very helpful. I used them, but found they were not working the way I wanted. At first they seemed to work well, but I found myself thinking, "there must be a better way...." so I went in search of better tools. The right tools made the work better, but preparing the soil still took work.

Preparing our soul for the seeds that God sows takes hard work as well. The tools which help cultivate our soil are called spiritual disciplines. We probably know about disciplines like prayer and reading Scripture, but there are others. You may find a discipline that works well. If so, stick with it. Allow God to use it. Maybe the discipline only works for a season. Allow God to lead you to other disciplines if need be. Spiritual disciplines are not "magic", but rather create space in our lives where God can work.

Are you practicing some kind of spiritual discipline daily? A garden needs tending and so does our soul. We tend our soul by creating space for God. Spiritual disciplines help create that space.

Take a few deep breaths. Allow God to breathe into your life. Ask him to lead you to disciplines that are life giving. Spend time thanking him for loving you just the way you are. Allow your desire for him to grow.

Your Reflections

Day 7 – Wednesday
Matthew 13:31-32

Preparing a garden takes time. My garden didn't go from a hard crusty shell to deep rich soil in an afternoon. It takes time to prepare the land, especially if the land hasn't been tended to. Wendell Berry wrote about 'reclaiming' land that had been uncared for. He said it took over twenty years to get the land the way he wanted it.

Previously, my garden was part of my yard. I mowed it, watered it, and did what anybody would do who wanted a nice yard. I can't imagine trying to create a new garden in an area that hadn't been cared for over the years. Preparing an uncared area would have been much harder and taken more time.

Tending the soil of our soul takes time as well. The time it takes to tend a garden discourages some people from ever having one. The time it takes to tend to a soul discourages some from that journey as well. Many believe they don't have time to pray, read scripture, or worship with others.

Some things are always worth the time. When we spend time in spiritual disciplines we develop a deeper relationship with God. Relationships, good ones at least, take time. Our relationship with God is worth the time.

Questions: Why don't I spend time in prayer, Scripture, or other disciplines? Am I really too busy? Do I not have the time, or am I spending it elsewhere? Has my soil become hard and crusty through neglect?

Allow God to lead you as you reflect. Spend time listening for God.

Your Reflections

Day 8 – Thursday
John 17:1-5

After working in my garden for a while, I began wondering why I was doing all the work. Salsa would be great, but I could buy salsa at the store for a few dollars. Was the work worth it?

While preparing soil for seeds was hard, the work didn't stop there. Gardens need constant tending. The work is not over once the soil is prepared and the seeds planted. To be honest, after a while, I was tempted to give up.

A garden takes perseverance and so does our soul. Our soul needs constant tending. Soul work isn't finished after we say "yes" to Jesus. There may be times when we want to give up our disciplines. We get busy and we don't believe we have time to spend in intentional prayer and Scripture reading.

When I wanted to give up working in my garden, the thought of great salsa motivated me to continue. What motivates us to keep tending our soul? Heaven? Growing in love and grace? Becoming who God has created us to be?

Jesus said to know God was eternal life (John 17:3). When we cultivate the soil of our soul, we grow in knowing Jesus. We don't just know him intellectually, we come to know him personally. The soul work you are doing draws you into God's presence and love.

Find a quiet place where you can limit distractions and spend focused time with God. Pray a prayer of openness and receptivity. Pray that God will help you to know him better through intentional practices. At some point this day, develop an intentional plan of prayer and Scripture.

Your Reflections

Day 9 – Friday
Luke 18:9-14

Prayer practice: The Jesus Prayer

The Jesus Prayer has strengthened Christians for over eleven centuries. The words of the prayer are quite simple but extremely powerful: "Lord Jesus, have mercy on me." A longer version of the prayer is, "Lord Jesus, son of God, have mercy on me a sinner." Some shorten the prayer to "Jesus, have mercy" or even "mercy." The words come from the parable of the tax collector in Luke 18:9-14.

The simple, biblical words of the prayer help us focus as we pray. The Jesus Prayer facilitates the practice of focused attention by giving us a way to be "called back" when we get distracted. The prayer is also considered a "breath prayer", meaning that as we inhale we pray, "Jesus, son of God" and as exhale we pray, "have mercy on me a sinner." If distraction breaks our focus, we simply go back to the prayer.

Set aside at least ten minutes. Spend a few moments taking some deep breaths in and out to release any tension. Begin praying the Jesus Prayer. Rest in God's presence as you pray. Allow God's spirit to fill you.

Your Reflections

Day 10 – Saturday

Begin by turning in your Bible to Luke 18:9-14 and slowly read the passage a couple times.

Think about the following:
1. What is happening in this passage?
2. Which person do you more closely associate with in this text?
3. When you pray, do you exalt yourself or humble yourself?

Pray quietly about last week. Thank God for meeting you and helping you prepare your soul to receive the planted seed. Thank God for softening your heart and your life over the past two weeks.

Your Reflections

The 2nd Sunday of Lent Day

Reading: John 3:1-17

Hymn: O God, Our Help in Ages Past
　　O God, our help in ages past,
　　Our hope for years to come,
　　Our shelter from the stormy blast,
　　And our eternal home!

Reflection: What part of this passage is familiar? What in this passage is new to you? What part of this passage is something that you needed to hear today? Spend some time thinking about God in your life and how you can find new life in Jesus today?

Prayer: Give thanks to God for all the help provided in your life. Celebrate that God wants to provide hope in the days, weeks, and years to come.

Your Reflections

Day 11 – Monday
Matthew 13:5-6

Read Matthew 13:5-6 and think about the image of seeds sprouting and quickly withering away.

You've probably seen the rock piles at the edges of plowed fields. Farmers pick up the stones one at a time and carry the heavy granite to the hedgerows and side-ditches. They know that every rock is an obstacle to growth for their crop.

Those with rocky gardens experienced the same truth: the seeds get fewer nutrients. They sprout, yes, but they do this of their own accord, like a bean wrapped in wet paper towel for a 5th grade science project. But to grow, to truly flourish and produce fruit, they need nutrients that they can't get from a garden filled with debris. The Seeds spread by the Great Gardener cannot grow deep when the garden of our soul is cluttered with the debris of Anger, Bitterness, Pride, Jealousy.

What clutters the garden of your soul? What keeps the Good Seed of God from taking root in your spirit? Do you struggle with envy of others' belongings; well-maintained cars, expensive houses, exceptional children?

Do you have pain in your heart and life as a result of others' words and deeds and you hold it close like a security blanket? Do you take pride in the fact that you are independent, needing no one to assist you in life?

Are the roots going deep in your heart and soul or is the debris keeping them at the surface?

Take a moment to pray that God will open the eyes of your heart to those things that keep you from truly trusting him and allowing the roots of God's Word to go deep.

Your Reflections

Day 12 – Tuesday
Philippians 4:10-20

The concept of the seven deadly sins was developed in the 5th century by John Cassian. One can think of the seven deadly sins as rocks in our soul. Pride, Envy, Greed, Anger, Acedia, Gluttony, and Lust keep God's seeds from flourishing. As you reflect on these rocks over the next few days, allow God to begin moving them out of your garden. We begin by reflecting on envy and greed which keep us from the joy of God's gifts.

Throughout Scripture we learn that God blesses. God does and has blessed us. If we know that God blesses, why are we so unsatisfied?

Envy causes us to minimize how God blesses us. Once we "look over the fence" we forget about *our* blessings. Focusing on what others have, whether it be material, relational, or some other aspect of life, diminishes how we view the gifts God pours into our lives.

Greed causes disappointment with how God blesses us. Greed wraps around our heart and chokes out joy. God's blessings are amazing and God gives us what we need, yet greed cries, "More, more, more!" Greed finds no satisfaction. There's never enough. We end up dissatisfied.

The balance to envy is contentment. Paul writes that he has learned to be content whether he has much or nothing. The counter to greed is generosity. When we practice generosity, greed loosens its hold on us. Generosity frees us and brings joy! Ridding our garden of these two rocks allows God's joy to flourish! We are blessed and that is enough!

Reflection: Are rocks of envy and greed in your garden? Spend some time reflecting on the gifts God has given you; friends, family, shelter, food, love, forgiveness, your church, and more. If you are discontent or disappointed, ask God to give clarity as to why.

Your Reflections

Day 13 – Wednesday
Philippians 2:1-13

Our second two rocks are pride and acedia. Pride may be a difficult rock to find because it hides itself. Even when we believe pride is not an issue for us, it may subtly take root fooling us into believing it doesn't exist.

Pride wears many costumes. Sometimes pride dresses itself up in self-criticalness. We criticize ourselves so that others might come to our defense thus stroking our ego. Pride also comes when we believe our ideas are the best, or that we could do the task better, or we get upset with the group decides to go in a different direction than we want.

Humility combats pride and brings true assessment recognizing that God uses both our talents and limitations. Humility is truth. It serves as a doorway to spiritual health and many spiritual masters believed humility was the most important virtue.

The desert fathers called acedia the "noonday devil." Some translate acedia as sloth or laziness which misses the spiritual element of the word. Acedia is laziness concerning our spiritual life. Acedia causes us to give up spiritual disciplines and put our spiritual life on "autopilot."

There will be times when we grow weary. We may wonder if we are making any progress in our spiritual journey. We will be tempted to give up. Acedia discourages us from continuing.

Passion for God combats acedia. Even when we are weary and feel we are not receiving benefit from our spiritual disciplines, worship, or community of faith, we continue out of love and passion for God. Spiritual masters like St. Teresa of Avila and John of the Cross continued to be faithful even when they no longer felt the presence of God. Their faithfulness revealed a depth of faith rather than a lack of faith.

Questions: At what times have I felt weary and ready to give up? Am I going through one of these "dry" periods now? What does it mean that God is with you even when you might not sense his presence?

Your Reflections

Day 14 – Thursday
Galatians 5:16-21

We end our survey of the seven deadly sins by looking at the rocks of gluttony, lust, and anger. Gluttony, usually viewed as over consumption of food and drink, can also be over consumption in general, which our culture tends to encourage.

Sex sells and fuels our culture. Yet, lust in the garden of our soul creates a hard surface making spiritual depth difficult. It isn't that God cannot penetrate deep into our lives, but that lust creates an atmosphere of death (James 1:13-15) rather than life.

Anger burns within us. It takes hold and doesn't let go. Have you ever been so angry you broke something? Or, perhaps you've said something you didn't really mean and later regretted?

We move these stones through self-control, purity, and forgiveness. These are heavy stones and we need God's help to remove them. Self-will only gets us so far. Usually these rocks begin innocently, but take a hold of our hearts sometimes quite quickly. Before we know it, these rocks take us to places we don't want to go. For some of us, removing these rocks may take a lifetime and only with God's help and power.

As we create space in our lives for God to work, we find, over time, these rocks become lighter. As we become open to God's presence and influence in our lives, we notice our reactions and attitudes changing and, slowly, the rocks having less and less impact. In their place is the wonderful harvest of God.

Questions: How might God help you remove these rocks? John Wesley talked about Christian Perfection as being perfected in love. Spend some time with God reflecting on how these rocks may inhibit your ability to love.

Your Reflections

Day 15 – Friday
Psalm 104
Prayer Practice: Nature

One way that God reveals his love and grace to us is through nature. God's fingerprints are everywhere. The Psalmists use nature as a way to connect with God.

While we may not usually think of it as a spiritual discipline, a great way to spend your time with God is surrounded by nature. This prayer practice uses your hiking shoes (or whatever shoes you have around). If the weather permits, find a place where you can walk and/or sit that is surrounded by nature.

Take a few deep breaths and allow God's spirit to fill you. God's handiwork surrounds you now. He is revealing himself to you through his creation. Allow God to speak to you through creation. What is God saying through the beauty that surrounds you? The variety? The sounds? The smells? Allow God to lift your heart in worship because of his beautiful creation of love.

Your Reflections

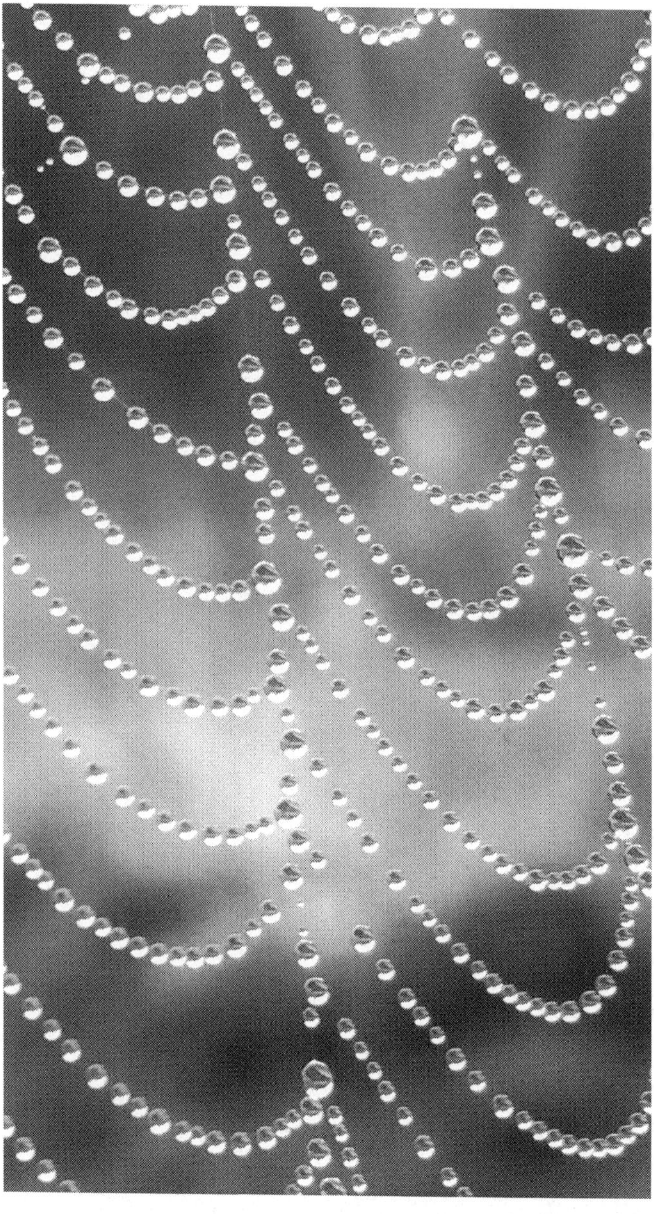

Day 16 – Saturday
Matthew 13:1-3

When I was a boy, we were told that we needed to give up something for Lent. I can't say we were ever told why this was required of us but it was clear that good Christians would follow this pattern...AND, we were expected to tell our fellow youth group attendees what it was that we were going to live without for the next 40-days. Some were going to sacrifice TV. Others were willing to go without rock music. Most of us listed essentials to life; like chocolate, bubble gum, or soda. The more mature and very few in our group reported that they were going to stop being selfish or stop lying (which I think was their first lie of Lent). While those were all good answers, I could only think that the one thing I wanted to give up for Lent WAS Lent.

It was hard to wrap my pre-teen brain around the idea that God loved us so much that he asked us to give up chocolate in order to better serve him. Like I said, the concept may not have been explained to us fully.

Of course, today I know that just as the Season of Lent allows us to focus on the sacrifice that Jesus made for us, the practice of self-sacrifice serves as a similar reminder. In fact, for many centuries, the Christian Church has utilized the practice of self-denial to highlight this truth.

Take a few minutes to think about the sacrifice that God has made for you, through giving his son, Jesus to die. How does that make you feel? How do you respond? How is your life a reflection of that great sacrifice and what do you do on a daily basis to respond to that gift?

Your Reflections

The 3rd Sunday of Lent

Read: Romans 5:6-8

Hymn: Alas! and Did My Savior Bleed
　　Alas! and did my Savior bleed,
　　And did my Sovereign die?
　　Would he devote that sacred head
　　For sinners such as I?

Reflect: It's often said that Jesus died to save the entire world. It is also said that Jesus would have died even if it were to save only one person. Isn't it wonderful that both statements are true? And what is more wonderful is that you are the one person. You are the one. In all your brokenness, in your pain, in your weakness...Jesus died for you. Think about that reality. Allow that good news to rest in your heart all day today.

Prayer: Bless you, sweet Jesus. Bless you for allowing your sacred head to be wounded for one such as I. Bless you, dear Lord.

Your Reflections

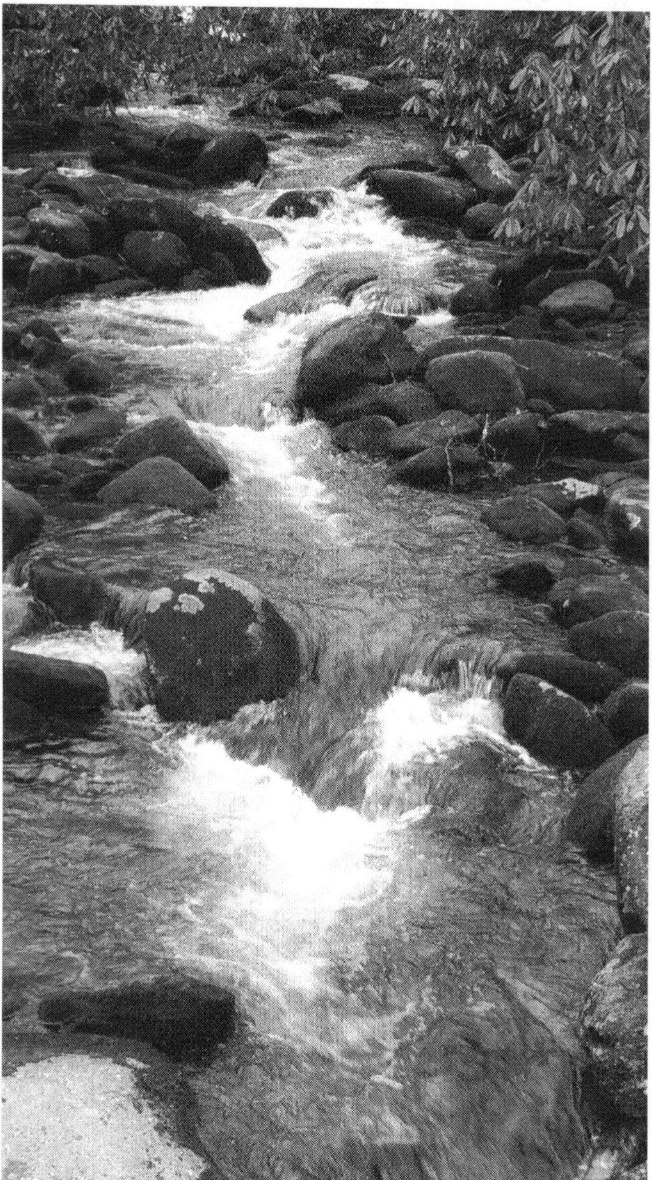

Day 17 - Monday
Matthew 13:24-30

My brother-in-law is a farmer. One day we were talking about pesticides and herbicides. He paused, looked me in the eye, and said something that will stay with me the rest of my life, "A weed is only a plant growing in the wrong location."

He's right! I want grass to grow lush and green in my yard and I spend a lot of time and money in an effort to make this happen. But when grass grows in the cracks of my driveway, it is nothing more than an annoying weed. I want raspberries to grow at the edge of my yard so I can enjoy the delicious fruit each year. But when these thorn bushes find their way into my garden or my yard, they prevent me from tending the fruit, yard, or vegetables.

The same is true with our lives and the weeds that can grow in our soul. In the right place, at the right time distractions like watching the game, catching up on the news, entertaining ourselves with movies, social media, and family commitments can be appropriate.

However, if we are not careful, those same things can take root in every aspect of our life. We can hyper-focus on sporting events. We can develop poor boundaries when it comes to family commitments. We fail to think of anything but our own entertainment.

Thankfully, if we are to allow the Seed of the Great Gardener to flourish, and keep those weeds in check, we can to ensure that these things don't become weeds that choke out the truth of God's love growing in us.

Read Matthew 13:7. Here we see that those thorns actually choke out the good seed. They take over and prevent the Good Seed from producing a good crop.

Take a few moments and pray about your life. Ask God to show you those things that receive more attention than they deserve. Ask God to reveal the "thorns" in your own life.

Your Reflections

Day 18 – Tuesday
Judges 6:11-18

Fear can be a weed taking our eyes off of God. Remember Peter? Peter walked on the water...until he started looking around (Matthew 14:22-33). Like cartoon characters who walk in mid-air until they realize what they are doing, Peter did pretty well for a while. When he looked at the storm, fear seized him. Peter sank.

The Bible addresses our tendency to operate out of fear rather than faith. Whether it is Peter walking on water, Moses going before Pharaoh, or Gideon hiding from the Midianites in the winepress, God's message continues to be "Fear not, for I am with you."

We sink when fear grows. Fear is wrongly focused faith. Fear focuses on the bigness of our problems rather than the greatness of the One who is with us. The thorns of fear choke out the life of God.

What is your greatest fear? Spend some time reflecting on where God is in your fear. Is God with you or do you feel all alone? Ask God to speak into your fear. Hear God speak into your life to "Fear not, for I am with you."

Your Reflections

Day 19 – Wednesday
Mark 1:35, Matthew 14:23, Luke 6:12

I was talking to a mother after a December "Kids day out" event. The event allowed parents to Christmas shop without their children. I asked, "What did you do with the time you had?" She responded, "I took a shower."

Parents of young children know how luxurious a shower can be. Parents are pressured to give their children every opportunity possible. Not only do sporting and school events crowd their calendars, there are also fundraising and leadership expectations as well.

You do not need to be a parent to know the pressure of work, church, and community organizations, not to mention spending time with family and friends. Time becomes an elusive and valuable commodity. A commodity, at times, we wish we had more of.

We live in an over-connected and over-committed world. We wear our over-commitment and busyness as a badge. We run from one event to the next. We eat on the run and we pray on the run. We pray while showering, brushing our teeth, or driving to work. We multitask God into our lives. It seems normal. If we weren't so busy, others might think we are lazy, or perhaps, unimportant. What choice do we have after all? We have to do these things? Right?

While any kind of prayer is good, even prayer on the run, if this is our only practice, we miss intentional focused time with God. The weeds of business infect our garden and steal nutrients from our soul.

Spend some time doing a "time inventory." Over the next few days write down how you spend your time. What are you saying "yes" to? What are you saying "no" to? Remember, when we say yes to one thing, we say no to something else.

Your Reflections

Day 20 – Thursday
Mark 10:1-20

We all have dreams and regrets. And if we are not careful, our dreams and regrets can become weeds and thorns that strangle God's life from us.

Regret causes us to live in the past. We go over what we did, or didn't do, again and again in our mind. Sometimes we become defined by the past and stuck there. Thankfully, whether it be past sins or missed opportunities, God continues to pull us forward in forgiveness and purpose. We need not live in the past, but can fully embrace God's present purpose.

Dreams and speculations cause us to live in the future. We spend our time planning and strategizing. While not having any plan isn't wise, there's a possibility that we are so focused on what may happen or what we want to happen, that we miss God's present reality.

The past is over and the future does not exist. God is with us now. Being stuck in the past or having our head in the future may cause us to miss God's present opportunities and possibilities.

The weeds of regret and thorns of speculation take root and grow blocking our ability to connect with the moment. We miss moments with our family, friends, and even ourselves, but we also miss moments with God.

Use this time to spend in God's presence allowing the thoughts of the past and future to simply pass by. Don't address them. Don't dwell on them. Simply allow them to pass. Spend time listening for God to speak into your present. Sense his love, grace, and forgiveness washing over you. Hear him speak words of comfort. He is with you...right here...right now.

Your Reflections

Day 21 – Friday
Jeremiah 29:10-14

Prayer Practice: Practicing the Presence.

Brother Lawrence was a 17th century monk who was assigned kitchen duty at his monastery. This would be an undesirable duty for most of us. Who really enjoys working in the kitchen cleaning pots and pans? Brother Lawrence might not have liked the work either, but he discovered that as he cleaned the pots and pans, peeled potatoes, or prepared meals, he could focus on God's presence.

Brother Lawrence discovered the truth that God is always with us and that means he is with us in the present moment. He would write that his time washing pots and pans was a time of worship better than any cathedral could provide. He documented his experience in the book, "The Practice of the Presence of God". We strongly encourage you to find this small book and add it to your spiritual reading.

After spending some time reflecting on the scripture passage for today, head into your day remembering that God is with you. As you go from task to task remember that the presence of God is in that moment, no matter how mundane or routine.

Your Reflections

Day 22 – Saturday
Judges 1:7-8

Have you ever struggled with quiet time? Have you ever tried praying and reading your Bible only to be frustrated by a lack of meaningful results?

It's a common experience, especially when first starting. Many find that developing the habit of effective and meaningful daily devotion takes practice. The right setting, the right time, the right passage to study all factor in to beneficial devotion time.

Thomas Edison is credited for creating the light bulb 1879, but, did you know that electric lighting devices were in development as early as 1803? Consider this, 75-years passed from the first glowing wire to the fully realized light bulb. That's 75-years of tinkering, trials, errors, successes and disappointments. Edison is quoted as saying that all those prior attempts were not failures to finding the answer to the light bulb. "I have not failed. I've just found 10,000 ways that won't work."

The ongoing effort to grow deeper in your relationship with God will require daily attempts at discipline; prayer, reading, quiet time. Some of these will be successful. Some will not.

Take a few minutes to think about your spiritual journey. Reflect on your greatest successes and your biggest challenges.

Ask God to meet you today and to help you to find the best way to prepare the soil of your soul. Read today's passage slowly and spend some time with God.

<u>Your Reflections</u>

The 4th Sunday of Lent

Reading: Ephesians 5:8-14

Hymn: Fairest Lord Jesus
   Fairest Lord Jesus, Ruler of all nature,
   O Thou of God and man the Son,
   Thee will I cherish, Thee will I honor,
   Thou, my soul's glory, joy and crown.

Reflection: Think of a time when you've been in the dark. Perhaps it is when the electricity went out during a storm. Simple tasks, like reading or writing are difficult when you are in the dark. Do you remember the relief you felt when the power returned and the lights blazed again? How did you feel in those moments?

Prayer: Thank God for shining light into the world, that we can see all things clearly, including his love and power active in our lives.

Your Reflections

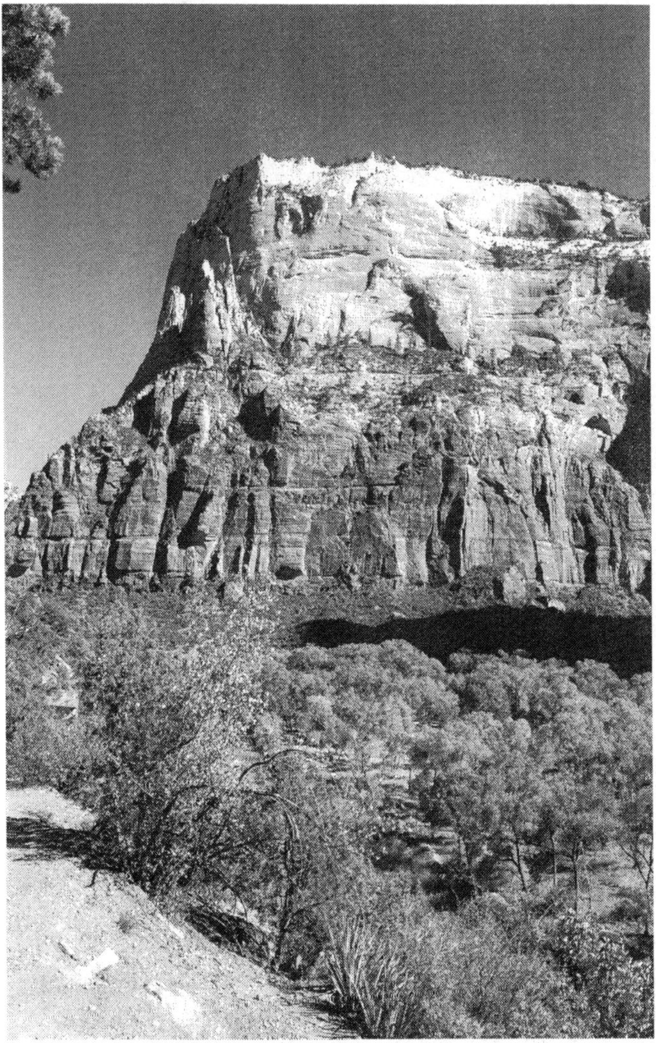

Day 23 – Monday
Matthew 7:24-29

One day I was complaining about my tomato plants to a farmer. I couldn't figure out why they were dying. "How often do you water them?" he asked. "I water them every day," I replied. He then told me, "That could be the problem."

He said watering my tomato plants every day wouldn't allow the roots to grow deep to find water. Instead, they would grow right beneath the surface. When the sun begins beating down, plants with shallow roots can die. When the sun beats down, and wind and storms come, deep roots are vital. He suggested watering periodically so the roots would grow deeper.

Jesus says plants that lack deep roots wither and die when trials comes. The question isn't whether trials would come, but will we be able to stand up under trials when they do come. Trials make and break us. Trials rise up and expose the depth of our roots. When our roots grow deep in God, we face trials knowing that God is with us.

Do trials tend to "set you off"? When trials come, what is your first response? Do you fall apart? Charge forward? At what point, if any, are you able to let go of the trial and give it to God? How might you cultivate a conse of trust in God's faithfulness?

Your Reflections

Day 24 – Tuesday
Psalm 3

I am not an expert gardener. Most of my discoveries have been by trial and error, talking to farmers, and watching YouTube videos. One thing I discovered is that deep roots are important, at least for tomato plants. While the plants can grow with shallow roots, the deep roots will see the plants through storms, drought, and high wind.

We also experience storms, droughts, and high winds in our life. Life throws quite a few curve balls at us. We may have hopes and dreams, but sometimes those hopes are lost in an instant. Dreams can be crushed just as easily. How do we stand up under trials and difficulties? How can we not just survive, but thrive under trials?

Deep roots in God help us stand. Deep roots enable us to continue to grow even through trials. Deep roots keep us connected to the Great Gardener of our soul.

Questions: Spiritual disciplines help us grow deep and keep us connected to our Great Gardener. Practicing disciplines cultivate a sense of God's presence in good times and bad. Can trials also help us to "grow deeper?" In what way?

Your Reflections

Day 25 – Wednesday
Philippians 4:4-9

Deep roots help us to thrive in the midst of storms. Deep roots also bring a harvest of God's joy, peace, and love.

Our culture focuses on finding happiness. We see this focus in commercials, TV shows, and movies. People make decisions based on whether the decision will make them happy. Our constitution gives us the right to "pursue happiness." But what if, satisfaction doesn't come through happiness? What if we finally get what we believe we want, happiness, but discover that it isn't what we really need?

Deep roots bring joy. Happiness is based on circumstances. When something good happens, we are happy. When something bad happens, well, happiness leaves as quickly as it came. Joy sticks around. Joy continues even when happiness walks out the door. Joy comes when we cultivate God's presence in our life. Joy comes as our roots grow deep.

Deep roots also bring peace and love. Jesus said his peace was different than what the world offers. We can have peace even when our world falls apart. Paul called it the peace that passes understanding. Along with peace, we learn that the love of God through Jesus sticks with us no matter what!

Joy, peace, and love come together as our roots grow deep in God. These deep tendrils keep us "rooted" in God's presence even when the storms, droughts, and winds try to uproot us. As we cultivate a garden that is free of rocks, weeds, and debris, our roots grow deep into God's presence.

Questions: Do you focus more on happiness (good things happening) or joy? Do you have peace in the midst of storms? Is God's love your foundation? How might joy, peace, and love be cultivated in your life?

Your Reflections

Day 26 – Thursday
Ephesians 2

The first time I tried to plant a garden, I was amazed. I started in late February, but since the weather wasn't conducive for plant growth, I decided to use an indoor greenhouse.

The kit came with compacted dirt that expanded with water. Each seed went into its own container. Every day I would look at the plant and for a while, I didn't see any progress. I wondered if my plan to start the plants inside would even work. But then, I saw a sprout.

I couldn't see was happening beneath the surface. Roots were growing. Each day they were growing deeper and deeper. One reason I had to finally move the plants outside was so the roots would have room to grow deeper than the containers allowed. If I would have kept the plants in the small containers, they would not have produced much, if any, harvest.

We need deep roots as well. Deep roots don't happen overnight. Deep roots take time.

Living in an instant culture makes us impatient. Just about anything we want or need we can have almost as soon as we want it. Spiritual formation doesn't happen in an instant. It takes time for our roots to grow.

We may minimize things that takes time, or give up because we sense a lack of progress. Prayer, Scripture, worship, service, all take time to provide full benefits and outcomes. We are tempted to give up these practices because we don't see "results". Yet, these practices help our roots grow deep below the surface. These practices open our lives so God's presence can flow.

Have you given up, or set aside spiritual practices because you didn't believe there was progress? If you have, what do you believe will help your roots grow deep?

Your Reflections

Day 27 – Friday
Psalm 1

Prayer practice: Lectio Divina

Lectio Divina is a Latin phrase that means "divine reading." The practice dates back to the early centuries of the church. Lectio Divina combines prayer and Scripture in a way that transforms us.

Western culture teaches us to master whatever we read. Through school we learn that tests follow reading. We study and, at times, cram so we can pass the test. We master the material in order to succeed.

Instead of mastering the text, Lectio Divina helps us to be mastered by the text. We slow down and allow the text to be both teacher and mentor. Rather than knowing the material, our goal is to be transformed.

There are four "movements" to Lectio: Reading, Meditating, Conversation (prayer), and Contemplation. We begin with prayer asking God to speak to us during this time and seeking to quiet our souls and become receptive to God.

Reading: We first read the text slowly noticing any words of phrases that "bubble up" from the text. We read the text a second time, a third time, and a fourth. Each time we read we notice the words or phrases bubbling up. The purpose of this movement is to slow down so we can hear God speak through God's word.

Meditating: Meditating literally means "Chewing the cud." We've seen cows chew cud. We chew on the words that have 'bubbled up' during our reading. Allow them to move in your mind. Wonder, why these words?

Conversation: We pray. We ask God, "Why these words? What are you seeking to speak into my life?" Sometimes we are surprised. We may think we know why the words bubbled up, but all of a sudden, clarity comes and God takes us in a different direction.

Contemplation: We sit. We sit with God. We sit with God's word to us. We sit in God's presence and commit to living out God's word.

We encourage you to find a book, or website on Lectio Divina. Practicing Lectio Divina can transform your life through Scripture and prayer.

Find a quiet place. Set an alarm for twenty minutes. Practice Lectio Divina using Psalm 1.

Day 28 – Saturday
Psalm 19

The Psalmist paints a beautiful picture of praise and activity in the sky. The day declares his wonder. The night shouts out his beauty. The writer of the Psalms notes that these objects have no voice and yet they proclaim the wonder of the Lord. It happens day and night.

The sun, moon, and stars have it right! Today is a good day to do praise God; whether the sun is shining bright or gray clouds loom, it is the perfect day to Praise the Lord.

When was the last time you celebrated God's goodness? When was the last time you thanked God for his power and grace?

Look out the window. What is the current weather? Sun or clouds? Light or dark? Heat or cold? Dry or wet? Think about the weather. Look up to the sky. Where is God in the midst of this?

Read the Psalm and allow your own praise to rise in your breast. Celebrate God's goodness in every season and focus on the writer's final words. How do your words and your own meditations please the Lord and praise his name?

Your Reflections

The 5th Sunday of Lent

Reading: Hebrews 5:7-10

Hymn: O Love divine, what hast thou done!
   The immortal God hath died for me!
   The Father's co-eternal Son
   Bore all my sins upon the tree.
   The immortal God for me hath died:
   My Lord, my Love, is crucified!

Reflection: Make a list of things you are thankful for today. List as many things as possible. This can be something as simple as the comfort of your chair or as complex as the love you receive from family and friends. Where does the passion and death of Jesus fall on that list? How has this one act in history impacted your life today?

Prayer: Spend the next few minutes thanking God for these gifts in your life and for his great sacrifice that gives life and breath to your very soul.

Your Reflections

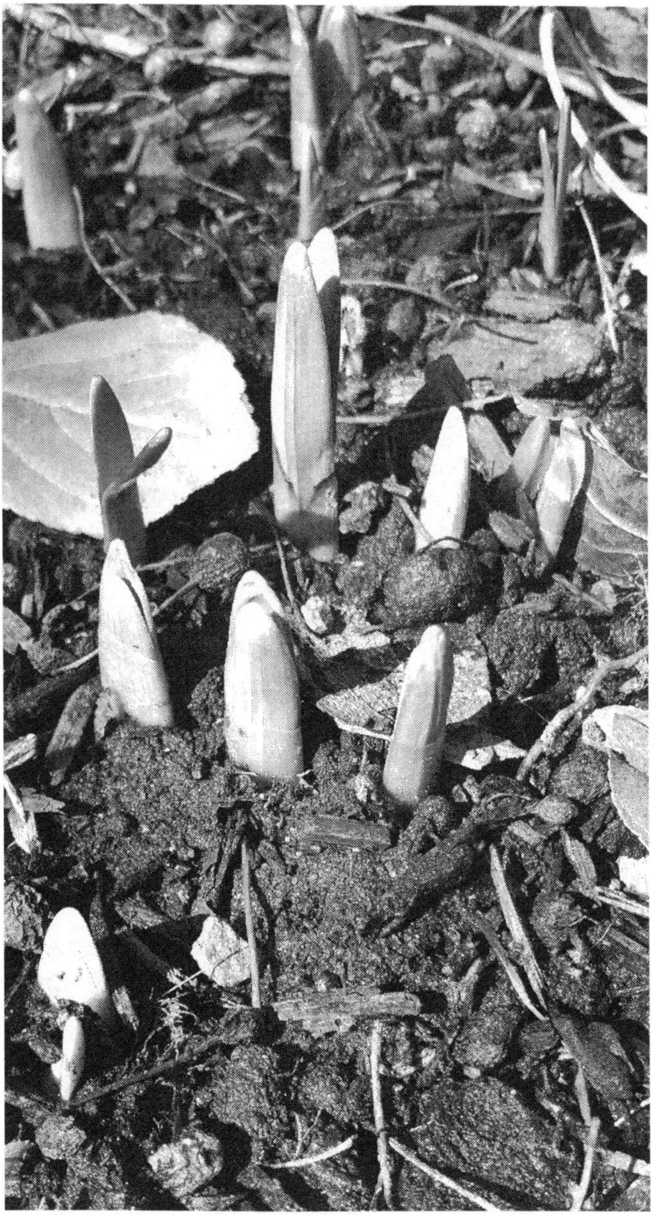

Day 29 – Monday
Genesis 1:26-31

We are created in God's image. God has planted himself within us. Our task is not to sow the seeds of God's presence; they have already been sown. Our task is to cultivate the soil to be conducive to growth.

Genesis 1:26 says, "Then God said, "Let us make humankind in our image, according to our likeness..." We have been created in the very image of God, but that image was deformed through sin. Through spiritual disciplines, we create space for God to work and restore his image. Even though we believe we are cultivating the soil of our soul, in fact, God is the great Gardener of our soul. We don't have to plant the seed, only give the seed good soil in which to grow.

The desert fathers used three states or ways to describe the progress of growth in our spiritual lives; purgative, illuminative, and unitive. Over the next three days we will reflect on these ways.

Questions: Reflect on being made in the image of God. How does having God's image at the center of your being impact you?

Your Reflections

Day 30 – Tuesday
Hebrews 12:1-13

The purgative way describes our first movements toward God by taking the rocks and weeds in our life seriously. I would say this is a time of purging. We purge those elements of our lives that obstruct growth in God.

When I first became a Christian, I sensed God calling me to 'let go' of some practices and attitudes. Paul writes in 1 Cor. 13:11, that when he was a child he acted like a child, but when he grew up, he put away childish things. I felt a lot like Paul. There were areas of my life that seemed to work well before I knew Jesus, but afterward, I knew God was calling me to "put away" those things. The purgative way had begun.

I won't go into detail about what my "things" were. My issues are not your issues. My calling is not your calling. We all have issues. We all have a calling. Our work is allowing God to lead us away from 'childish things' into new life with him.

We all go through this time of purging. No one is perfect. All are forgiven. God leads us to places of healing, blessing, and new life. We cannot hang on to the old while embracing his newness. To embrace God's life in us, it means we must let go of the old life of self.

Your Reflections

Day 31 – Wednesday
2 Corinthians 5:16-21

Genesis tells us that God created man and woman in his image. Theologians refer to the "*Imago Dei*" which is Latin for "image of God". You and I were created in God's image. We all have God's image within us. You may find this hard to believe, but you are God's masterpiece. I am too! We are the *Imago Dei!* Paul says Christ in us is the "hope of glory!" (Col. 1:27)

Genesis also tells us that something went terribly wrong. Sin entered and marred God's beautiful masterpiece. Mother Teresa once said that those she served were "Jesus in disguise." While God's image is within each of us, sin disguises God's beautiful creation. This is true in my life and in yours.

The seed planted within us by the Great Gardener, is none other than God's Image! It seems incredible because we are so used to seeing the 'outside' that has been disguised by sin.

We do not plant the seed…God has already sown the seed. Our part is to rid our "garden" of rocks and weeds so God's seed might grow in the best possible soil. Cultivating good soil has been the focus of the last few weeks.

After the purgative way, we find ourselves in a place of growth. In the illuminative way God's light shines in our lives and our eyes and lives are open. We have removed rocks and weeds. God's presence begins to flourish. The new has come! Yes, there are still some weeds and a few rocks, but the soil is getting better each day.

During Lent you have been meeting with God each day. How will you allow God's light to shine in your life when Lent is over? Are there practices that God is leading you to? Find one other person who can help keep you accountable as you journey on the illuminative way.

Your Reflections

Day 32 –Thursday
Philippians 3:12 – 4:1

The past few days we have looked at the purgative way and the illuminative way. The spiritual masters believed the deepest path in the spiritual life was unitive way or union with God.

While we are all invited to have our wills united with God, very few individuals reach this stage of transformation. In the unitive way, our wills become coalesced with God's. Our minds are focused on God's will. Peace characterizes our lives and our desire is God.

John Wesley taught that we could be perfected in love. I see parallels in Wesley's focus on being prefect in love and the saints focus on being united with God. The ultimate goal of our life in God is love. We are called to a union of love.

As we cultivate the soil of our soul and God's presence flourishes within us, the harvest produced is love. Not human self-interest and self-referenced love, but a God and other-referenced love centered in God.

Jesus told his disciples that they were to love as they have been loved (John 13:34). How is your love? Are you able to love others the say way Jesus has loved you? Are you growing in love of others? Spend time in Jesus' love. As you head into your day, allow his love to flow through you. Paul writes that even though he is not perfect, he presses on to "make it my own" (Phil 3:12 ESV). Are you pressing on?

Your Reflections

Day 33 – Friday
Luke 4:1-13

Prayer Practice: Fasting.

Fasting has traditionally been viewed as going without food. John Wesley believed fasting was an important practice and encouraged all Methodists to fast. Wesley's practice was to fast on Wednesdays and Fridays.

For some, health reasons prevent a full fast. If you have health issues, there are still opportunities to practice modified fasts by giving up certain foods, drinks, or spices. John Wesley wrote about only eating "plain" food as a modified fast.

There are still other ways to fast: Giving up electronics, social media, TV, or certain types of entertainment creates time and opportunity that can be used for other purposes such as prayer, spiritual reading, or service. Letting go of attitudes and practices can be a way to fast as well.

The practice of fasting isn't really about what we give up. A regular practice of fasting reminds us that what we need more than anything else is God and God's presence.

The pangs of desire we sense as we fast are a reminder that while we are physical creatures with important physiological needs, our deepest needs cannot be fulfilled by a burger and shake, Facebook and Twitter, or judging someone. Unmet desires are a cue to move our focus and attention off of the "less than" and onto the "more than."

For this practice today, seek to fast from distractions so you can give your attention to God. If a thought comes, simply "let it go." Don't think on it, don't address it as "good" or "bad." You are not your thoughts. Thoughts come. This practice is letting thoughts go, so you might be fully attentive to God.

Your Reflections

Day 34 – Saturday
Mark 10:46-52

Begin the day by praying that you will be able to be honest with God about the state of your heart, the condition of your soul. Take a minute to let God touch you, love you, and renew you.

Read the passage in Mark. As you read the story, consider each person, what they see and what they do.

First, think about blind Bartimaeus. How do you think he felt calling out for help? What was it like to have everyone tell him to be quiet? What was it like to have everyone support him in his quest to see…to see Jesus? What was it like for him to see for the very first time? What was the first image he viewed? Wasn't it Jesus, the healer?

Think about the crowd. Why did they rebuke Bartimaeus when he called for help? Why did they change their mind and help him find Jesus? What story did they tell their family and friends for years to come about what they witnessed that day?

Think about the disciples. What are they thinking? What are they seeing? Isn't it interesting that they are not mentioned at all in the passage beyond walking with Jesus? Why is that? Or were they among those rebuking Bartimaeus?

Finally, think about Jesus. How many people called out to him that day? How many wanted to know his touch? How many needed healing? What do you think he thought as this blind man persistently reached out to him for help? How did Jesus feel when Bartimaeus opened his eyes for the first time?

Spend the remainder of your time imagining the scene and all that happens there. Meditate on the words that are not recorded, the emotions we can only imagine, and the sights, sounds, and smells of that amazing day.

How did God move in that moment? How is God moving in your life today?

Your Reflections

Introduction to Holy Week

We've made it to Holy Week. This is a special week in the life of the church. It can be a special week for us as well. We can choose to spend this week like any other, or we can set it apart as a *holy* week. We can use this week as a way to identify with Jesus' life, suffering, and death.

St. Ignatius believed that God could speak to us through our imagination. Ignatian prayer uses our imagination so we can enter the story of Scripture. This method of prayer works best with the Gospels. Through our imagination we enter into the scene. We might find we are Peter warming his hands, or a soldier who is trying to arrest Jesus. We notice the sites, the sounds, the smells, and the emotions of the event. This method does not concern itself with analyzing the text (you can do that in a Bible study later), but rather experiencing the text.

The Ignatian Spirituality website states, "Contemplating a Gospel scene is not simply remembering it or going back in time. Through the act of contemplation, the Holy Spirit makes present a mystery of Jesus' life in a way that is meaningful for you now. Use your imagination to dig deeper into the story so that God may communicate with you in a personal, ovocative way."[i]

As we approach Good Friday, and ultimately Easter, try using Imaginative Prayer to enter into the events surrounding this week. This way of prayer may be difficult at first. All practices, spiritual or not, are difficult when we begin, so don't become discouraged. Remember that the desire to please God, does in fact please God as Thomas Merton observed.

You can find more information at the Ignatian Spirituality website referred to in the notes at the end of this guide.

The 6th Sunday of Lent
HOLY WEEK
(Passion Sunday)

Reading: Luke 19:28-40

Hymn: O Sacred Head, Now Wounded
    O sacred Head, now wounded,
    With grief and shame weighed down,
    Now scornfully surrounded
    With thorns thine only crown:
    How pale thou art with anguish,
    With sore abuse and scorn!
    How does that visage languish
    Which once was bright as morn!

Reflection: The people of Jerusalem celebrated the entry of the King. They did not fully understand the sacrifice this King would make for them. Now that you know the sacrifice of Christ, do you celebrate or do the rocks still need to cry out His praise?

Prayer: Repeat and meditate on the following: "Thank you, Jesus, for freely giving your life for me."

Your Reflections

Day 35 – Monday

Prayer Practice: Ignatian Method of Prayer

This is Holy Week. For our prayer practice we imagine walking with Jesus during this week. Imagine the sights, sounds, and smells. Imagine yourself as a bystander, disciple, Pharisee, or even Jesus.

Before reading the Scripture, ask God for grace as you read through the passage twice. Read slowly. Become part of the event.

Luke 19:41-44

As Jesus draws near to Jerusalem he pauses and prays. One can almost sense the pain in his prayer. During his ministry, Jesus invited people to follow him. A few did. Most did not. Imagine the sadness and disappointment as he looks over the city and people he loves and realizes they missed God's invitation to life.

As you place yourself in this scene, listen to God. What do you most identify with? What do you feel? Talk with God.

Your Reflections

Day 36 – Tuesday

Before reading the Scripture, ask God for grace as you read through the passage twice. Read slowly. Become part of the event.

Read: John 12:20-36

Jesus learns that some Greeks would like to see him. This seems to trigger something within Jesus. His mood changes. He becomes reflective. This event seems to indicate that Jesus' end is near.

Notice Jesus' words, "Now my soul is troubled. And what shall I say? 'Father, save me from this hour?' But for this purpose I have come to this hour. Father, glorify your name..."

Enter into Jesus' pain. Place yourself into the scene. Allow God to speak into your life.

Your Reflections

Day 37 – Wednesday

Before reading the Scripture, ask God for grace as you read through the passage twice. Read slowly. Become part of the event.

Read: Matthew 21:12 - 17

"Blessed is he who comes in the name of the Lord!" the crowd shouted. People grabbed palm branches and started waving them. People cried out praises to God.

Palm Sunday was quite a celebration. For the disciples there must have been joy unspeakable. For three years they followed Jesus and now, finally, things were coming together.

By Good Friday the cries of praise turned to cries of "Crucify him!" Perhaps it was a different crowd, or maybe, Jesus began doing things that caused the people to reassess their view of him. Whatever the reasons, within a week, the climate surrounding Jesus changed drastically.

What part do you play? Where are you in this event? Talk with God.

Your Reflections

Day 38 – MAUNDY THURSDAY

Before reading the Scripture, ask God for grace as you read through the passage twice. Read slowly. Become part of the event.

Read: John 13:1 - 20

Allow your imagination to place you in the scene. Who do you most identify with? One of the disciples? Peter? Judas? Jesus?

Or, simply stand outside the episode and observe the scene. What do you notice? What do you feel?

Allow God to speak through this Scripture.

Your Reflections

Day 39 – GOOD FRIDAY

Before reading the Scripture, ask God for grace as you read through the passage twice. Read slowly. Become part of the event.

Matthew 27:32-59
Luke 23:26-49
Mark 15:21-41
John 19:16-30

Choose one of the scriptures above. Find a quiet place. Take some deep breaths in and out. Jesus is here with you. He has been waiting for this time because he wants to meet with you. He wants to talk with you.

Begin with prayer. In your own words, tell Jesus that you want him to speak into your life. Tell him you are open and receptive to what he wants to say to you through the Scripture passage. Give God your attention and ask him to lead your imagination.

As you read through the passage, slowly, allow God to lead your imagination. What is your mind drawn to? Are there sounds? Smells? Allow the crucifixion to become real to you. What do you most identify with?

    Spend time in conversation with God.

Your Reflections

Day 40 – HOLY SATURDAY

Prayer Practice: Silence and Solitude

The cries of crucifixion are over. Jesus is dead. What has happened, has happened. What will be, is unknown. There is only silence in the tomb.

This day reminds us of the silence of the grave. We all live in an "in between" time. What will be, we do not know. All we know is that Jesus is dead.

Resurrection seems far away. "What we will be has not yet been revealed," writes John (1 John 3:2). "We see through a glass darkly," Paul reflects (1 Cor 13:12). We look forward to what will be: Resurrection.

You have spent 47 days with Jesus in prayer, reflection, and focus. Spend this day in quiet reflection. Allow the silence to be an inner silence of your heart. Even in the busyness of your day, remember the silence of Jesus' grave.

Your Reflections

EASTER SUNDAY

Before reading the Scripture, ask God for grace as you read through the passage twice. Read slowly. Become part of the event.

John 20:1-22

The tomb was empty! Jesus is alive! This is a day of celebration!

Over the past 48 days we have reflected on God's word. We have addressed the rocks, weeds, and shallow soil in our lives so that the soil of our soul would produce a harvest! We may not have even realized that *we* were coming forth from the grave! New life is here! We are alive. The old is gone, the new is coming (2 Cor. 5:17). We are a new creation. We are alive!

As you read the Scripture, enter into this event through your imagination. Remember, resurrection is your story too.

Talk with God.

Your Reflections

REFERENCES

All photography © C. Curtis Austin

I Am Thine, O Lord – Words by Francis Jane Van Alstyne. Public Domain.

O God, Our Help in Ages Past – Words by Isaac Watts. Public Domain.

Alas! And Did my Savior Bleed – Words by Isaac Watts. Public Domain.

Fairest Lord Jesus – 17th Century German Hymn. Public Domain.

Love Divine - Charles Wesley. Public Domain.

O Sacred Head Now Wounded – Benard of Clairvaux. Public Domain.

---

[i] (http://www.ignatianspirituality.com/ignatian-prayer/the-spiritual-exercises/ignatian-contemplation-imaginative-prayer)

Made in the USA
Charleston, SC
22 January 2016